thegpsgirl's
Road Map
for
Your Future

Put Yourself in the Driver's Seat

Karen Jacobsen
the gps girl®

Dedication

To Thomas & Anita Jacobsen who have
always been my greatest cheerleaders

and

To my husband Tom who makes me feel
as if I can do anything.

Table of Contents

About The GPS Girl

Karen Jacobsen was born and raised in Mackay, near Australia's Great Barrier Reef and moved to New York City on July 4th, 2000. She refused to listen to warnings she would "grow out of it" and pursued her childhood dream to be a Professional Singer and Songwriter. Releasing seven records on her label Kurly Queen, Karen's music has taken her around the world, on to network television and in to sports stadiums where she has proudly performed anthems at national and international events.

Karen relocated from Mackay to Brisbane and then to Sydney where she "fell into" Voice Over work during the 1990's, booking literally thousands of commercials. In 2002 she went on to audition in New York City for a client needing "a Native Australian Female Voice Over Artist living in the North East of the United States."

Almost fifty hours of recording later, Karen's speaking voice ended up in GPS units in over 25 million cars in four major brands around the world giving directions to drivers. Making the connection between directions in cars and directions in life, she created "The GPS Girl".

Passionate about loving her own life, she shares how she overcame chronic insecurity and navigated her way from the Great Barrier Reef to the Big Apple. "The GPS Girl" writes, sings and speaks to groups who want to inspire the best in their people and create a road map for their future. She absolutely adores living in Manhattan with the two loves of her life, her husband Tom and son Hayden.

Preface

There is an epidemic sweeping the globe. Ask just about anyone; "What would you love to do if you could do anything?" and nine times out of ten they will say "I Don't Know."

I believe everyone knows.

We just need to hear ourselves through the noise of life.

Planning a dream future is not generally part of the curriculum of formal education and living a life we love is seldom encouraged.

Even if you think you are too old, too tired, too poor, too everything under the sun to start planning what you would really love to do, *now* is the time.

We aren't very good at creating a road map because we hardly ever do it. Choosing college classes, planning a wedding and preparing for the arrival of a baby are some of the obvious experiences when we really prepare. We know our destination and we start making decisions.

When else in life do we write out our goals and plot our glorious future?

It's such a simple step and one many of us manage to avoid.

We have a 90% better chance of our dream future happening, just by writing it down.

Let's practice so we can excel at it.

Introduction

I love to write out my goals and read them.

I can spend hours doing this and I am always collecting ideas for what I would love to do in my future, how I'd love to be in my future and what I'd love to have in my future.

I fill journal after journal with my plans and it thrills me when something I have written down happens in my life.

My wish for you is that the journal you have in your hand provides the inspiration to put pen to paper and create a road map for your dream future.

On every level, from the smallest daily task to the most extravagant dream come true, allow yourself to imprint the ideas in your mind onto the page.

These are some of the tools I have used to navigate my way from the Great Barrier Reef to the Big Apple and to live a life I absolutely love.

I love lists.

To me they are excellent "Directions for Life".

In the pages ahead I've included many of the lists I have created for myself.

Why do I find them so useful?

Because when I wake up in the morning I need reminders of where I am headed.

Creating a Road Map for Your Future is just the first step.

Looking at that Road Map every day is the real key.

Please have fun with this process. Drink your favorite cup of tea, coffee or champagne as you write. Listen to music you adore as you ponder the experiences you'd love to have.

Carry this journal with you so you can add to it any time. I recommend adding to it every day. Really.

Write down the first thing that comes to mind.

Use a pencil if you must.

Let's not wait another minute to create a Road Map for Your Future.

Chapter One

The Driver's Seat

We live as if life is happening to us. It can seem as if we have little or no influence on how things turn out and we are merely at the effect of it all.

What would it be like to experience being in the Driver's Seat of life?

When I was twenty-four years old I was introduced to the idea I could have some control over creating my future.

I started to live like things were really possible. I started to think I had something to do with achieving my goals. It started to feel a lot less like a lucky coincidence when things went my way.

We may not always have a choice about what is happening to us, but we *always* have a choice about our experience or how we react to what is happening.

That's right, we always have a choice about our experience.

This is the magic of how to be in the Driver's Seat, by taking charge of how we react to every little thing that happens in our daily life.

When challenges show up, ask yourself "Am I in the Driver's Seat or the passenger seat?"

I feel in control when I am in the Driver's Seat. Like I have taken charge. Like I am on top of things. What it means is I am experiencing living my life proactively instead of passively.

Being in the Driver's Seat I feel like a 'make it happen' kind of girl.

Being in the passenger seat can be fun. Going along for the ride in life and letting someone else do the steering has its place as long as you know this is what you are choosing. How wonderful to be able to support someone else. However being in the passenger seat can also be waiting for it to happen.

Why I want to be in the Driver's Seat is to feel free, passionate, purposeful and joyful in simple moments, all day every day.

Being in the Driver's Seat is a conscious choice.

Are you going along for the ride or taking charge?

Chapter Two

Inner GPS

As a little girl, many well-meaning adults would ask the question: "What do you want to be when you grow up?"

I would proudly answer "a Singer and an Actress."

Many would laugh, snigger (that's Aussie for snicker) and tell me I would 'grow out of it.'

I did not grow out of it.

For a seven-year-old girl it was painful to have adults laugh at my dream. You see, I knew from a young age what I wanted to be when I grew up.

It was crystal clear.

Somehow I knew how to listen to my Inner GPS; that voice inside that said:

"Somebody has to be a Professional Singer, why not me?"

"This is what I am meant to do."

…and then it started to say

"I'll show them."

There are times when you know you are in exactly the right place at the right time with the right people doing what you are born to be doing.

That's when you are listening to your Inner GPS, your inner wisdom, your heart.

What Is My Inner GPS and How Can I Find It?

Think about the times in your life when everything was flowing and everything was working. The times when you felt totally integrated.

You were listening to your Inner GPS.

There's a good chance you were doing what you love most and experiencing tremendous joy.

Then there were the times you knew something was a bad idea, you did it anyway and had to deal with the consequences.

If everyone around you is telling you which way to go and your Inner GPS or your heart is screaming at you to do something else, always follow your Inner GPS.

It will steer you the right way.

Sometimes I can't tell which way to go because I don't have a strong feeling or instinct about it.

So I wait and I listen. Until I know it is right.

Here are some of the times I listened to my Inner GPS and things worked out brilliantly:

- Leaving Australia to move to New York City.

- When I knew I was meant to marry my husband.

- Traveling to Zambia to meet my sponsored child.

- Pursuing music full time at the end of university.

Now it's your turn.

Times I Listened to My Inner GPS and Things Worked Out Brilliantly

How Do I Learn To Listen To My Inner GPS?

Quiet time.

Ideally, sitting still in a quiet space with your eyes closed, focused only on your breathing.

Even if you can only find two minutes in a day, it is enough to begin. Anyone can find two minutes in a day. That's right, even you!

Perhaps it's the last two minutes before you turn out the light at night.

A million thoughts may come and go, but as little as two minutes a day will make a difference.

You will start to hear yourself think.

You will begin to connect with the real you underneath the thoughts – the thoughts filled with a laundry list of things you haven't done and need to do (or just don't want to do.)

Try practicing next time you are in line waiting to order a coffee, or in the bathroom, or in the shower. The shower is the perfect place to wash your thoughts away and learn to listen to your Inner GPS.

Notice the thoughts come and go as you focus on breathing in and breathing out.

Be patient with yourself.

This is one of the kindest gifts you can ever give yourself and you will notice changes in a short period of time. Stick with it.

Ultimately, for best results, quiet time is at least twenty minutes per day.

It can be a major challenge and seemingly impossible to find twenty minutes. I'll bet you can find two minutes. Just two. I have broken it down so we can create a healthy habit.

Learning to Listen to My Inner GPS

If at all possible do this *first thing* in the morning.

If not, schedule it before noon so you don't find yourself at the end of the day grappling with "Will I just skip today because I am too tired?"

Perhaps, like me, you have a small child or a baby and first thing is not going to happen. Many times my meditation time is after my son is asleep in the evening.

Here's how I did it.

I made a deal with myself to take on a 30 Day Challenge and decided on a reward when I completed all 30 days.

The benefits in wellbeing and peace of mind were tremendous anyway, but I found having a reward to be a great incentive when I had a case of the "I Don't Feel Like It's."

The reward could be a massage or even something material you would love that would be a real treat.

- Sit comfortably in a quiet space
- Set a timer
- Close your eyes
- Focus on your breathing
- As thoughts come, let them go

That's it.

You now have a meditation practice.

Can you believe how easy this is?

You just began to infinitely reduce your chances of every major disease out there and immeasurably improve your quality of life.

There Is No Such Thing As Doing It Right

If there are *lots* of thoughts, you are doing it right. If there are none, you are doing it right.

Sit and be still.

If you are sitting quietly with your eyes closed, focused on your breathing, you are doing it right.

There is no mystery formula. For years I thought I wasn't doing enough and I felt I definitely wasn't doing it right.

How could sitting quietly while focused on my breathing possibly work? There wasn't enough hard work and effort involved, was there?

If you meditated for two minutes a day for a year instead of nothing, you would notice a world of difference.

Let me know if you are taking it on.

Inner GPS 30 Day Challenge

I am taking on the Inner GPS 30 Day Challenge.

beginning

_____, the ____ day of _____,

and completing

_____, the ____ day of _____,

for at least _____ minutes per day.

My reward will be

_____

Signed by

_____

Date

_____

Chapter Three

Destination

The first step toward getting what we really want is deciding. Simple enough, but it's amazing how indecisive we can be.

Not deciding is another way of proving to ourselves that we "don't know what we want". We're going to break it down.

1. Choose a destination.

2. Take steps toward it.

3. Recalculate when necessary.

Here is the most beautiful part about choosing a destination when creating a road map for your future. It is an ever-changing, ever-flowing work in progress. You are not married to it.

You can and will make changes to it all the time.

Where are you headed?

Where would you love to be headed?

I think part of our reticence to going for what we really want, or allowing ourselves to even contemplate what that could be, is the thought we may choose the wrong thing and be stuck with it.

What if we do make a wrong decision?

What if we don't love our dream destination when we arrive?

What if we get what we think we want and we are still not happy?

This kind of thinking is just another distraction.

Let it go.

Allow yourself to want what you really want. Think, "If I had a magic wand, how would my life be?"

Perhaps you'd love to be filled with joy going to work every day.

Or to feel completely comfortable in your own skin.

It could simply be to feel good at all.

Put aside all the considerations and rules you have created about how life should be, and ask yourself again:

If I had a magic wand, how would my life be?

"It's the journey, not the destination" I hear you cry.

I agree, but it is having the destination in mind that contributes to the experience of the journey.

What we expect is going to happen can bring fear or joy, so I find it a lot more enjoyable to plot my desired destination and enjoy the ride.

When I was seven years old I saw Olivia Newton-John on television and my life changed.

I knew I wanted to be a Professional Singer and move to America. There she was, a blonde Australian singer and actress who had traveled to the U.S. and was welcomed with open arms.

I had no idea how I was going to be just like her, but I knew it was my destination.

Choose a destination.

Take steps toward it.

Recalculate when necessary.

If I had a Magic Wand

If I had a Magic Wand

_____

_____

_____

_____

_____

_____

_____

_____

_____

_____

_____

_____

_____

_____

_____

_____

_____

_____

When I Grow Up

For a moment we are going to pretend.

Turn back the clock to a time when you were seven years of age.

Anything you want to do with your life is possible.

What do you want to be when you grow up?

You may already be doing what you love.

However, if you are still wondering what that could be, here is a place to start.

Write down whatever comes to mind.

When I Grow Up

How I Love to Spend My Time

What do you absolutely love spending your time doing?

Where the time just evaporates and you completely lose track of how long it's been.

Put aside whether you can make a living doing it just for now.

You may love to hang out in restaurants with friends.

Perhaps you love entertaining, organizing, having picnics, traveling, reading biographies, problem solving, watching television, swimming or being with children.

Someone is making an excellent living right now doing the things you love to do.

How I Love to Spend My Time

The Times I Feel the Most Joy

The only reason we want any of the things we want is we think it will bring us joy.

- We want a million dollars and

- To find our true love and

- To travel to exotic places and

- To be fabulously successful

All because we think it is going to bring us exquisite joy and happiness.

Chances are the things that bring us the most happiness are simple and already available, regardless of our current circumstances.

Let's expand on the things that are already working in our lives.

The Times I Feel the Most Joy

Chapter Four

Directions

We are giving ourselves directions every moment of every day. Every thought we think is like a direction.

"It'll never happen."

"Why bother."

"I am not good enough, tall enough, rich enough, thin enough, young enough."

It's time for some directions that will lead us toward the destination of our dreams.

You've probably heard of affirmations.

They are phrases that affirm good and positive results.

We are actually using counterproductive and negative affirmations constantly whether we realize it or not. Just revisit the phrases above.

When we say an affirmation aloud or write it out, we are creating a future we are designing.

I don't know about you, but my default setting is to beat myself up.

Through using affirmations, reading inspiring books and surrounding myself with energized, purposeful people, I spend less time than ever feeling bad about myself.

It still happens but my bounce back time is much faster.

When I start my day with an affirmation like "I love my life", I set myself up for a vastly different experience than if I use "I am so tired."

At first it can really feel like a case of "fake it until you make it".

What would it be like to handle any little detour, roadblock or setback that happens by being able to brush it off?

How would it feel to be able to stay focused on your destination and proceed with confidence and vitality?

Affirmations have worked wonders for me.

Here is how they work.

Directions for Affirmations

1. Create a phrase that describes the kind of experience you would love to be having.

2. Feel great while you say the affirmation aloud or as you write it down.

   You may have to fake it until you make it.

3. Repeat the affirmations every morning and every night in the bathroom mirror.

   Start with just one.

   Try it.

   You may feel resistant, confronted, annoyed or perhaps excited as you proclaim your affirmations out loud.

Some of my favorites I use again and again.

- I am being totally taken care of

- I am always in the right place at the right time

- I am successful, accepted and loved

- Great things are happening for me

Start by writing a list of words you love and then create your own affirmations.

It is essential to remember to feel good as you say them.

Words I Love

My Affirmations

_____

_____

_____

_____

_____

_____

_____

_____

_____

_____

_____

_____

_____

_____

_____

_____

_____

_____

Chapter Five

Lists as Directions for Life

Lists are like directions we give ourselves and they are a major part of our road map.

Let's take a daily routine as an example.

What elements make up a great day?

A truly fabulous day?

We all know there are things that would be good for us, for our health, our wellbeing and our state of mind, but we don't always do them as consistently as we could.

There are experiences we really look forward to. There are people we love being with, especially when we have fun plans with them.

Fill your calendar with these kinds of appointments!

If you are not having fun in life and can't remember how long it's been since you really, really laughed, it is time to put yourself in the driver's seat and start scheduling fun.

Many more of the everyday things feel fun when we feel good.

Let's work on ways to feel good, feel better and put the spark back into life.

Lists give us an opportunity to plan one step at a time. One foot in front of the other. That's as complicated as it needs to be.

Perhaps you would love to jump out of bed each morning filled with joy, gratitude, energy and vitality.

It's just a series of steps away.

Every step we take is a step in the right direction.

The Spark Plug List

Write a list of things you could do each day that would really impact how you feel.

Ways to be your own spark plug.

Here are some of mine.

- Drink a full glass of water first thing

- Choose my clothing the night before

- Repeat an affirmation

- Have something beautiful I see as soon as I wake up

- Take a few deep, focused breaths

- Take vitamins

- Meditate. As little as two minutes a day makes a difference

- Stretch. Start with just one gentle stretch

- Make a call to say "I love you"

- Perform a random act of kindness

My Spark Plug List

I Love Lists

Here are some of the lists I use to move all the swirling worry out of my head. I would much rather it be on the page.

- My Purpose

- My Priorities

- Top Ten High Priorities

- Daily Directions

- Weekly Directions

- Monthly Directions

- Love Love Love List

- Breakdown List

- Budget (Some feel better calling it a Spending Plan)

- Net Worth

- Recalculating

- Refueling

- Spark Plug

- Morning Routine

- Evening Routine

and the really fun lists

- Directions for my Dream Day

- This Year I Will…

- Fun Projects

- People I Would Love To Meet

- Books I Have Been Meaning To Read

- Gifts I Would Love to Receive

- Gifts I Would Love to Give

- Celebrations I'd Love to Plan

- Holiday Destinations of my Dreams

- Adventures

- Qualities I am Developing in Myself

- The Times I Feel the Most Joy

- What I Love Most About My Life

- How I Love to Spend My Time

- Dream Dates

- What I Appreciate Most About My Life

- Ways I Can Serve By Doing What I Love

and

- My Road Map. The top 100 things I would love to be, do and have in my future.

There is plenty of room on the pages ahead to ponder these lists.

As my good friend Mark LeBlanc says, "Done is better than perfect".

This statement has changed my life.

Once upon a time I would not start things if I thought I wasn't going to be able to do them perfectly.

There are a lot of projects I didn't start. Now I get on with it.

This journal is a great example. I would rather provide a place for you to write down your dream destinations in life than keep striving for some idea of perfection that doesn't actually exist.

This is an exploration, so let's explore!

I Love My Life

What would it be like to love everything about your life? Everything you do, eat, drink, every person you spend time with, everything you wear?

Imagine loving it all.

The person who is in charge of this would be you.

A long time ago I decided I would only buy something if I truly loved it. This makes shopping so easy!

Everything I have in my home I love. How long has it been since you cleared out the clutter in your home and life?

Try removing things that you do not love and create the space for something new.

I live a life I love. Every part of it.

Life is not perfect nor do I strive for it to be.

I get upset and disappointed, but I no longer wallow in my own self-pity for extended periods of time.

Every decision I make, I make out of love.

I ask the question "Do I love it?"

What I Love Most About My Life

Directions for My Dream Day

If you could have a Dream Day, how would it go?

Who would be with you?

Where would you be?

What would you do?

Where would you dine?

What would you be thinking at the end of your Dream Day as your head hits the pillow?

My Dream Day

How I Would Love to Feel

How does your Dream Day make you feel?
What is the experience of being there?

You are in charge of your experience right now. Incorporate the feelings you would feel on your Dream Day into today and tomorrow. Even if it doesn't seem like it, you are the person in charge of the way you feel at all times.

My Purpose

What do you feel you were born to do?

It probably includes some of the ways you love to spend your time.

Are you born to serve, love, inspire, create, share, educate?

Are you here to you use your passion, creativity, joy, exuberance, enthusiasm, patience, empathy, precision, calm nature, humor, love, attention to detail?

Do you want to make the world more peaceful, caring, connected, efficient, easy-going, happy, loving, fun?

Remember, done is better than perfect.

Write down some ideas. Make a start.

Give it a go.

My Purpose

_____

_____

_____

_____

_____

_____

_____

_____

_____

_____

_____

_____

_____

_____

_____

_____

_____

_____

Priorities

What is most important to you?

Above all else.

Explore by writing as many priorities as you can think of and we will become more selective in a moment.

Knowing our priorities makes things crystal clear.

How to spend our time.

How to spend our money.

What to do first.

What really makes us happy.

My Priorities

_____

_____

_____

_____

_____

_____

_____

_____

_____

_____

_____

_____

_____

_____

_____

_____

_____

_____

Top Ten High Priorities

Daily Directions

Things I like to make sure I do on a daily basis.

_____

_____

_____

_____

_____

_____

_____

_____

_____

_____

_____

_____

_____

_____

_____

_____

Weekly Directions

The most important things I like to do every week.

If I've Got This List Handled, I Feel On Top Of Things In My Life

_____

_____

_____

_____

_____

_____

_____

_____

_____

_____

_____

_____

_____

_____

_____

_____

_____

Monthly Directions

Each month I would love to be able to achieve and
experience the following:

_____

_____

_____

_____

_____

_____

_____

_____

_____

_____

_____

_____

_____

_____

_____

_____

_____

Love Love Love List

_____

_____

_____

_____

_____

_____

_____

_____

_____

_____

_____

_____

_____

_____

_____

_____

_____

_____

Breakdown List

A list of all the annoyances in life.

The things you do not look forward to and frankly do not want to deal with.

Start by walking around your entire living space and write down the things you find irritating that need fixing,' improving and replacing.

Take a mental inventory of the experiences literally sapping joy and energy.

Include things that are a bother or a constant worry.

Perhaps conversations you are putting off or dreading.

You could choose to tackle one thing on the list every day, week, month, or jump in the deep end and go for it on all fronts.

There may be actions to take from this list but by simply writing them down and knowing you have them documented, space will open up.

My Breakdown List

_____
_____
_____
_____
_____
_____
_____
_____
_____
_____
_____
_____
_____
_____
_____
_____
_____

Budget

(Some feel better calling it a Spending Plan)

Knowledge is power.

If you think a budget will restrict you I can tell you from experience it is the single most financially freeing action you can take.

Once you are clear on the high priorities in life and you know where the money goes, it's possible to redirect spending to where it will really bring joy!

This could be a whole separate book. Take a few minutes to make a start by writing a list of fixed expenses and discretionary expenses.

- **Fixed expenses** – the ones you know for certain are coming each month (rent, mortgage, utilities, etc.)

  and

- **Discretionary expenses** – the ones that change each month you have complete control over (groceries, eating out, entertainment, clothing, shoes, shopping)

My Beautiful Budget

Spending Plan

_____

_____

_____

_____

_____

_____

_____

_____

_____

_____

_____

_____

_____

_____

_____

_____

_____

Net Worth

Everything you OWN minus everything you OWE.

_____

_____

_____

_____

_____

_____

_____

_____

_____

_____

_____

_____

_____

_____

_____

_____

Enjoy the Ride and Remember to Refuel

Our whole lives are a reflection of how we feel about ourselves, which is why it is extremely important to feel good.

Enjoy every step on this journey and set up rewards along the way.

Write a list of ten rewards you would love.

1. _____

2. _____

3. _____

4. _____

5. _____

6. _____

7. _____

8. _____

9. _____

10. _____

Is this one of the most challenging lists to write? You really do deserve to be rewarded. Make them big, small, simple, detailed; make them rewards you would absolutely adore.

Write some more.

Refueling

A list of ways to reward myself for no reason at all.

_____

_____

_____

_____

_____

_____

_____

_____

_____

_____

_____

_____

_____

_____

_____

_____

My Morning Routine

My Evening Routine

_____

_____

_____

_____

_____

_____

_____

_____

_____

_____

_____

_____

_____

_____

_____

_____

_____

_____

This Year I Will...

_____

_____

_____

_____

_____

_____

_____

_____

_____

_____

_____

_____

_____

_____

_____

_____

_____

_____

_____

Fun Projects

People I Would Love To Meet

Books I Have Been Meaning to Read

Gifts I Would Love to Receive

Gifts I Would Love to Give

_____

_____

_____

_____

_____

_____

_____

_____

_____

_____

_____

_____

_____

_____

_____

_____

Celebrations I'd Love to Plan

Holiday Destinations of My Dreams

Adventures

Qualities I Am Developing in Myself

_____

_____

_____

_____

_____

_____

_____

_____

_____

_____

_____

_____

_____

_____

_____

_____

_____

_____

Dream Dates

Whether single, dating, engaged or married, this list can completely transform life.

What I Appreciate Most About My Life

_____

_____

_____

_____

_____

_____

_____

_____

_____

_____

_____

_____

_____

_____

_____

_____

_____

Ways I Can Serve By Doing What I Love

Chapter Six

Recalculating

I believe we can recalculate any time in life, just like we can in our car.

Life is one big recalculation.

We have a plan, but that plan changes all the time. Sometimes it changes daily. This is perfectly ok.

When we hear the word "Recalculating" from the GPS when we are driving, there may be a moment of irritation or we may even make ourselves wrong for being off route.

Recalculating is *good news!* It means you are now back on track.

The word recalculating is supposed to bring comfort. It is designed to give us reassurance.

Even though we may think we know exactly how things will turn out, we are recalculating all day every day.

Things don't go exactly as planned and we make adjustments. Think of it as an opportunity for a do-over.

The times I know I most need to be recalculating?

- When something doesn't go as planned

- When I am upset

- When I am annoyed

- When I am frustrated

- When I just "Don't Feel Like It"

Here's how I shift gears to get back on track or to recalculate.

When I notice I'm getting grumpy (or if someone points it out to me) I do a quick check and ask myself the following questions.

- Am I hydrated?

- When did I last eat?

- Am I well rested?

- Am I breathing deeply?

If the source is one or more of the things on this list I can interrupt my level of drama pretty quickly.

We are simple creatures and some of the basics are usually missing if it is not going well.

Here are some of the ways I use to recalculate and get back on track.

- Play music I love

- Make a cup of tea

- Buy myself flowers

- Take five slow deep breaths

- Take a walk around the apartment or around the block

- Call someone to let off a little steam

- Drink water

- Eat a healthy snack

- Get up and dance

- Write down three things I am grateful for

Create a list of ways you could recalculate. Include some you can use at the office, or in a public setting that are easy to implement.

What we are really after is a list of ways to shift the energy.

Make a copy of your recalculating list and carry it with you or put it where you can see it. Memorize it and *use it*.

Recalculating List

When Life Happens

Sometimes it is not quite that simple. Life happens. We can be broken hearted or dealing with extremely challenging circumstances.

If you are going to feel bad, go all the way there. There are times it is important to fully feel our grief, disappointment or heartbreak.

- Set the timer for an hour, a day, a week

- Pull the covers up

- Watch the saddest movie

- Cry it out

- Eat cookies and ice-cream

- Then brush yourself off and start again

Be intentional about it. Be responsible about it. (Don't drag everyone around you down just because you feel miserable.)

Be in the driver's seat and declare you are going to fully feel it before you move on.

It's called being human.

Chapter Seven

Creating a Road Map for Your Future

Start writing down all the things you would love.

- To be in your future

- To do in your future

- To have in your future

Just write.

How would you love life to be?

Add to this list every day.

Create it in glorious detail.

Be specific.

Be really specific.

If

If I knew I couldn't fail I would...

_____

_____

_____

If I knew I would be wildly successful I would...

_____

_____

_____

If I could be known for anything it would be for being...

_____

_____

_____

If anything could happen today, it would be...

_____

_____

_____

If I could go anywhere on an all expenses paid vacation I would go to...

_____

_____

_____

Chapter Eight

My Road Map

If you can dream it, you can create it.

It's just a series of steps on your Road Map.

Visualize!

Take a few minutes whenever you can in your day to literally daydream about the experience of arriving at your dream destination.

Picture yourself enjoying every minute of it. Really be there.

Feel the feelings you imagine you will feel when you are there.

If you'd like some inspiration while creating your very own road map, there is a luscious list of possibilities at the back of this journal.

I wish you so much love and fulfillment as you create and live the road map for your future.

My Road Map

1. _____

_____

2. _____

_____

3. _____

_____

4. _____

_____

5. _____

_____

6. _____

_____

7. _____

_____

8. _____

_____

9.

10.

11.

12.

13.

14.

15.

16.

17.

18. _____

19. _____

20. _____

21. _____

22. _____

23. _____

24. _____

25. _____

26. _____

27.

28.

29.

30.

31.

32.

33.

34.

35.

36. _____

_____

37. _____

_____

38. _____

_____

39. _____

_____

40. _____

_____

41. _____

_____

42. _____

_____

43. _____

_____

44. _____

_____

45.

46.

47.

48.

49.

50.

51.

52.

53.

54. _____

_____

55. _____

_____

56. _____

_____

57. _____

_____

58. _____

_____

59. _____

_____

60. _____

_____

61. _____

_____

62. _____

_____

63. _____

_____

64. _____

_____

65. _____

_____

66. _____

_____

67. _____

_____

68. _____

_____

69. _____

_____

70. _____

_____

71. _____

_____

72. _____

_____

73. _____

_____

74. _____

_____

75. _____

_____

76. _____

_____

77. _____

_____

78. _____

_____

79. _____

_____

80. _____

_____

81.

82.

83.

84.

85.

86.

87.

88.

89.

90. _____

_____

91. _____

_____

92. _____

_____

93. _____

_____

94. _____

_____

95. _____

_____

96. _____

_____

97. _____

_____

98. _____

_____

99.

100.

More Road Mapping

Inspiration

Feel comfortable in my own skin

Live in Italy for a year

Write a book

Fly my family to Hawaii for a vacation

Host a concert in my home

Run a marathon

Float in the Dead Sea

Make pasta from scratch

Visit the seven wonders of the world

Skydive

Learn a new language

Climb a volcano

Drive across the country

Be kissed under the mistletoe

Go to a drive in movie theatre

Bake a pie from scratch

Laugh until I cry

Swim in every ocean

Visit Stonehenge

Meditate in a Buddhist temple

Hot air ballooning

Build a tree house

See all of the nominated Academy Award movies

Ride a gondola in Venice

Be a contestant on Wheel of Fortune

White water rafting in the Grand Canyon

Visit Uluru

Drive on the Autobahn

Sing jazz in a black evening dress

Be an extra in a movie

Learn to ballroom dance

See the grand final of my favorite sport

Shower in a waterfall

Travel to all 50 of the United States

Skinny dip

Give blood

Enjoy a traditional 'high tea' at an elegant hotel

Love going to work every day

See the Northern lights

Ride a horse along a beach

Be able to express my feelings

Send a message in a bottle

Drive on Route 66

See a Broadway musical

Sleep in a tree house in the Amazon

Plant a tree

Visit the Pyramids

Set foot on every continent

Eat sushi in Japan

Climb a lighthouse

Plant a vegetable garden for the neighbors to use

Swim with a sea turtle

Fly in a private jet

Ride a mechanical bull

Walk the Great Wall of China

Take a trip on a steam train

Fly first class

Buy a round of drinks for everyone in the bar

African safari

Marry the love of my life

Ride an elephant in Thailand

Stay in the presidential suite

Travel the world

Cook a home-cooked meal with someone I love

Throw a coin in the Trevi Fountain

Cook Thanksgiving dinner

Visit the Taj Mahal

Write a poem for someone I love

Eat caviar and champagne

Enjoy great health

Ride a Harley Davidson

Take chances

Visit 100 countries

Visit the birthplaces of my parents

Conduct an orchestra

Be able to do a handstand without the wall

Go on a silent meditation retreat

Graduate from college

Swing on a trapeze

Feel successful

Fall asleep under the stars

Stay in an ice hotel

Cruise on the QE 2

Create a business that helps people

See Niagara Falls

Type 60 words a minute

Smoke a Cuban cigar in Cuba

Be able to sing my favorite song

Visit the ruins of Pompeii

Be willing to confront my fears and move through them

Circumnavigate the globe

Ride on a double decker bus

Vacation in an over the water bungalow in Bora Bora

Swim in the ocean at night

Romance with roses, candlelight and champagne

Own my own home outright

See an opera at the New York Met

Be someone who brings joy into people's lives

Fly a plane in a flight simulator

Eat strawberries and cream at Wimbledon

Tell the truth

Practice random acts of kindness

Make a big and anonymous donation to a charity

Raise a happy child

Bicycle down Mt Haleakala in Hawaii at dawn

Become a parent

Buy dinner for the people behind me in the drive-through

Walk along the Champs Elysees in Paris

Laugh every day

Take a husky ride in Alaska

Land on an aircraft carrier

Sponsor a child in a third world country then meet them

Take a surfing lesson

Live on the ship "The World"

Eat vegetables from my own garden

Build an enormous sandcastle

Open a holistic learning center

Make dinner on a campfire

Send my Mother flowers on MY birthday

Buy a brand new car

Make snow angels

Snorkel on the Great Barrier Reef in Australia

Learn my favorite poem by heart

Write in a gratitude journal daily

Volunteer to serve Christmas dinner

Purchase a gift in a little blue box from Tiffany

Parasail in the Carribean

Abseil

Have my Wedding by the water

Visit Easter Island

Crush wine grapes with my feet

Have my own TV talk show

Travel to Machu Picchu

Own a house by the lake in the mountains

Join the Peace Corps

Eat pasta in Sorrento on the Amalfi Coast in Italy

Create a website

Swim in the Blue Grotto on Capri, Italy

Watch the sunset from Santorini in Greece

Be truly fulfilled

Own my own jet and take my family and friends on trips

Climb Mount Everest

Write a will

Do without owning a car for a whole year

Meet my childhood idol

Sleep on the beach overnight

Cuddle a koala

Respect myself enough to take good care of my body

Trans-Siberian Railway

Volunteer to do conservation work on an off-shore island

Bungee jumping in New Zealand

Swim in a river

Hike the Appalachian trail

Barging on the canals in the United Kingdom

Play golf in Scotland

Sing "The Sound of Music" on an Austrian mountaintop

Wildlife tour in the Galapagos Islands

Be able to understand my Parents' perspective

Go on a family holiday as adults

Dance in the rain

Peking duck in Peking (Beijing)

Take a stand up comedy class

Build my dream home

Visit the outback of Australia

Sail on a tall ship

Go to the top of the Eiffel Tower in Paris

Test drive a Ferrari

Have my portrait painted

Enjoy a day at the races

Keep a journal

Witness a baby being born

Take a boat down the Nile

Arrange a surprise party

Appreciation

My love and thanks to Vali Bennis, Tara Clarke, Janice FitzGerald, Lyn Girdler, Heather Harmer, Tracy Kreutzer, Lucy Martinez, Glenda Nicholls, Alison Rogers, Kirsty Spraggon, Jennifer Watt and Stephanie Winters for sharing their own Road Maps.

To Rachael Bermingham, Sue Gilad, Terry Hawkins, Robyn Stecher and Robin Steinfeld for your "you can do it"-ness and to Donna McGovern, Misha Rubin, Rich Trincellito and Stephanie Woo for loving support.

My dear ones in Mackay, Brisbane, Sydney and elsewhere over the globe, thank you for staying with me.

To all the Jacobsens and all the Hudaks and especially Tom and Hayden who fill my life with the kind of joy even I did not think was possible.

Without Mark LeBlanc this journal would simply not exist. Thank you Mark for knowing what I am capable of before I know, and for so beautifully encouraging me to create and fulfill on the destinations of my dreams. I am deeply grateful.

And to you. Thank you for being someone willing to explore an inspired future. It takes courage. Lots of it. I would love to hear your victories and discoveries. If you would like to be in touch join The GPS Girl group on facebook or visit my website http://www.thegpsgirl.com